THIS BOOK IS DEDICATED TO
<u>CRAIG R. GATES II</u>
A BEAUTIFUL SOUL WHO CONVINCED ME, MY
ART BELONGED IN HANDS.
THANK YOU.

IF YOU THINK IT'S WRONG, IT WASN'T MEANT
FOR YOU
-ART

You have a right to your own feelings
But he's crying in my arms
And your laughing in his

I HATE THAT I ALLOWED MYSELF TO THINK I
DESERVED YOU

WE DON'T GRIEVE THE SAME
DONT COMPARE YOUR FEELINGS TO MINE
YOU DON'T KNOW HOW BADLY IT HURT
LIKE MY SKIN WAS BEING RIPPED FROM MY
BONES
LIKE I WAS DROWNING
MY MIND WAS COMMITTING SUICIDE EVERY
NIGHT
AND IF YOU HAD FELT A SINGLE SECOND OF
HOW I FELT FOR YEARS
YOU WOULDN'T BE HANGING UP HER STOCKING.
DON'T SHOVE THE PHONE IN MY FACE
I DON'T WANT HER ANYMORE
AND I HAVE EVERY RIGHT TO FEEL THAT WAY.

I TELL THEM THEY SHOULD CHERISH THEM
BECAUSE THEY DISAPPEAR SOONER THAN YOU
THINK
YOU SHOULD FEEL LUCKY YOU STILL HAVE THEM
BECAUSE SOME OF US
HAVE NOTHING AT ALL.

THEY COULD DISAPPEAR RIGHT BEFORE YOU
EYES
AND YOU'RE GOING TO TREAT THEM LIKE THIS?
WHAT WILL YOU DO IF THEY LEAVE
AND THAT WAS THE LAST THING YOU SAID TO
THEM

You didn't deserve to be treated like that.
I'm really sorry.
If I could curse the world for the things they did to you
I would.
If I could have done something to change it
Or at least make you forget.
I would in an instant
I wish your last moments weren't in a world that did that to you.
I will never forgive them
And that is a weight I'm willing to carry on my heart forever.

I HOPE THE MONEY YOU PROFITED OFF HER LIFE
WAS WORTH IT.
I HOPE IT GOT YOU A NEW CAR
MAYBE A NEW HOUSE
PERHAPS A DIAMOND RING
BUT I ALSO HOPE THAT MONEY FAILS YOU
I HOPE THE CAR BREAKS DOWN, WHEN YOU NEED
IT MOST.
I HOPE YOU CAN HEAR DISTANT SCREAMS
HAUNTING YOU IN YOUR HOME. I HOPE IT
DRIVES YOU INSANE.
AND I HOPE THAT DIAMOND RING RUINS EVERY
CHANCE AT LOVE YOU EVER GET.
AND I HOPE DEEP DOWN
YOU FEEL EVERY OUNCE OF PAIN SHE FELT
BEFORE SHE DIED.
I'VE NEVER WISHED EVIL ONTO ANYBODY.
BUT THAT WAS BEFORE YOU LET EVIL GROW IN
MY FAMILY.

I know it isn't fair for me to be angry
Trust me I do
I don't mean to make you feel guilty
I just hurt really badly
And the anger in my heart needs
somewhere to go
And I'd never say any of this to your face
No good will come from your pain
Despite what I used to think
You suffering wont help me
And your apology isn't needed for me to
heal
So I'll tuck everything away in this book
And pray you never open it.

HIS BAND MATE WAS KILLED IN A CAR ACCIDENT.
HE DID NOT CURSE THE MAN WHO DID IT OUT
LOUD
BUT YOU COULD SEE IT IN EVERYTHING HE DID
DAGGERS TUCKED AWAY IN HIS LYRICS
HE WAS ANGRY
HE WAS HEARTBROKEN
BECAUSE THAT WAS MORE THAN HIS BAND MATE
IT WAS THE LOVE OF HIS LIFE
AND SOMETIMES THERE ARE THINGS
WE SIMPLY CANNOT FORGIVE

He was nine when he had to start looking after his little brother. Making sure he got dinner and tucked into bed every night.

He was eleven when he had to start turning his dad on his side while he was passed out on the couch.

He was twelve when he had to start telling his mom "No", making sure she didn't gamble all the money they had.

He was thirteen when he had to start working a job in order to pay rent and buy groceries. He still had to go to bed hungry.

He was fifteen when he had to start fighting off his dad, desperate to keep him from breaking everything they owned.

He was sixteen when had to explain to his little brother their mom wasn't coming home, she ran away with a guy she met.

He was seventeen when he had to throw his father out of the house because he was too destructive.

And suddenly he was eighteen

He thinks "How is that possible? How am I grown if I was never allowed to be young?"

When I'm around you
It's hard to find love for myself
I feel inconvenient
Like I broke something I never touched
Did I ruin your life just by having one?
Am I wanted?
I didn't think I was this hard to love.

You were supposed to love me.

Let me bleed on the floor

My heart is breaking again
So desperate to be whole
I try to pull myself together
But there's something in the gravity
Because the pieces keep falling to the
ground
There's no other hands but mine to catch
them
But for some reason they go right
through my fingers
I don't know what happened to me

HAUNT ME.
I HAVE BECOME SO EMPTY,
I WILL ACCEPT ANYTHING OF YOU.

THE ONLY ONE WHO HAS HELD ME WHILE I FELL
APART
WITHOUT ME FEELING IMMENSE GUILT
WAS THE FLOOR.

I can't expect you to put out the cigarette
Toss the drugs
Dump the beer
Because even though I broke and lost
parts of myself I'll never see again
And I deserve for that to never happen
again
It wasn't just me
You were there too
Your heart broke too
And the only difference was
How we chose
And what we had
To fix ourselves
And I'm sorry
I'm sorry that was your only choice
I'm sorry that was the only thing you
found to save yourself.

I see you.

I FEAR THERE WILL ALWAYS BE A PIECE OF MYSELF
THAT REFUSES TO BELIEVE I AM CAPABLE OF
BEING LOVED.
THE MILLION OF REASSURANCES
AND I STILL DON'T QUITE GOT IT.
I RIDDLE MYSELF WITH OTHER MOTIVES AND
FALSE WORDS
TEARING MYSELF DOWN TO SOMETHING SO
INCREDIBLY SMALL, I DARE TO SHOW IT
KINDNESS.
THE LIES I TELL MYSELF ARE LIKE STEPS GOING
DOWN TO A STATE THAT LEAVES ME AWAKE AT
NIGHT EVALUATING EVERY MOTIVE AND MOVE
EACH STEP STEEPER THAN THE ONE BEFORE
I CAN'T SEEM TO STOP
I KEEP GOING DOWN
UNTIL ITS ME WHO IS INCAPABLE OF LOVE.

Why did I have to be so blind to something
that was within me?
It lived deep in me without a second of my
own thought.
I have caused tremendous pain
And have done nothing to save
Despite the cure being within myself.
I deserved all that pain you beared
I should have paid for every second of it,
for it was my own sin.
I deserve no resurrection
I deserve nothing
But to rot

What have I done?

You have laced my bones with yourself
And I have desperately tried to scrub them
clean
But I fear they are forever stained

I feel guilty
People always tell me you have to forgive
And I tried
I really did
But there are some things
Certain moments
That have never earned my forgiveness
There are some things so bad
My heart is too big to let go
It soaked up too much pain
And now it has to drown in all that
weight
The weight of hating you and what you
did
I proceed to hate myself for hating you
Not because you don't deserve to be hated
But because I don't deserve to suffer this
much for something I never did.

YOU DON'T SET A FIRE JUST TO WALK AWAY
YOU WILL WATCH ME BURN

They might have been little moments to
you
But they stuck with me
They twist my mind until I don't
recognize myself
They make me question my actions and
even my worth.
Those little moments jab at me whenever I
convince myself I deserved to be loved
Those not so little moments keep me up at
night, sitting in the dark as I take myself
apart piece by piece looking for the leak
Desperate to know why I am the way that I
am
And eventually I just settle with hating
myself, thinking there is no use in trying
to fix me because this is just how I am
All because of those little moments.

I'M SCARED TO BE FORCED INTO THE LIGHT.

When I am gone,
I'll only miss the world for you,
For you are the only true thing it has had
to offer
And in that,
You are the whole world.

I'VE SPENT YEARS BY MYSELF
SITTING ALONE AT LUNCH
NO STORIES TO SHARE
BUT I WAS ALRIGHT
I WAS CONTENT WITH MYSELF
FOR YEARS.

SO WHY CAN I NOT MAKE IT THROUGH THIS
NIGHT?

I MISTOOK A LEAF FOR A BUTTERFLY
AND FOR A MOMENT I WAS HAPPY.

I TRY TO IMAGINE YOU'RE HERE
I IMAGINE YOU'RE VOICE HIDDEN IN THE RUSTLE
OF THE TREES
I IMAGINE YOU SITTING IN REACH OF ME
I PICTURE YOUR FACE
BUT IT DOESN'T FEEL RIGHT
I SUPPOSE MY IMAGINATION HAS LIMITS.

I THINK I SHOULD WAKE UP A BIT BEFORE I
RESORT TO DRUGS.

HE DIDN'T RESONATE IN THE FACT THAT HE WAS
BROKEN.
HE DIDN'T LET HIMSELF SETTLE FOR LESS THAN
WHAT HE WAS DESTINED FOR.
HE TOOK THOSE SHATTERED PIECES
AND HE USED THEM IN THE ART
THAT SAVED HIS LIFE.

I UNDERSTAND SELF DESTRUCTION
I REALLY DO
YET THERE IS SOMETHING HURTING ME WHEN I
SEE THOSE TOWERS FALL WITHIN SOMEONE ELSE.

THERE ARE PEOPLE WHO ARE GOOD AT BEING
SAD
THEY'RE SAD A LOT
THEY FIND IT EASY TO SLIP INTO
AND I BELIEVE SOMETIMES THEY ENJOY IT
THEY FIND COMFORT IN THE STURDY FEELING
THEY EVEN SEEK THE STATE IN SEARCH OF
SOMETHING REAL
THEY WANT TO BLEED, JUST FOR A GLIMPSE OF
THAT CRIMSON COLOR
THEY WANT TO BREAK JUST TO REFRESH THE
PLACEMENT OF THEIR BONES, TUCKING THEM
AWAY, MENDING THE CRACKS
THEY WANT TO CRY SO THEY CAN SEE THAT NEW
SET OF EYES STARING BACK IN THE MIRROR,
SURROUNDED BY SHINY STAINED SKIN
THEY WANT THE PAIN TO RISE IN THEIR CHEST
AND THAT LUMP TO FORM IN THEIR THROAT
BECAUSE FOR SOME FUCKING REASON IT FEELS
RIGHT
THEY WANT TO FEEL
BECAUSE FOR THEM IT'S RARE

POETS PIERCED BY PASSION

I'm hungry for the kind of sleep I know I'll never have.

I FEEL SORRY FOR MY HEART
SHE BREAKS HERSELF
CHASING AFTER CARS SHE'LL NEVER CATCH
STRETCHING FOR STARS SHE'LL NEVER TOUCH
JUMPING WITH NO WINGS
AND LOVING WITH NO PROMISE OF ANYTHING
IN RETURN.

YOUR GUILT WILL NOT UNDO THE THINGS YOU
BROKE.
IT WILL NOT CLEANSE YOUR MIND OR EVEN
YOUR HEART.
THE CARPET IS STILL STAINED.
AND THEIR GRAVES STILL STAND.

MUCH LIKE THE SUN
YOU'RE BRIGHT, GOLDEN,
AND WARM AGAINST MY SKIN.

MAYBE THE REASON I'M SO SAD IS BECAUSE I FORCE THOSE MEMORIES TO MY ATTENTION, NO MATTER HOW HEARTBREAKING, BECAUSE THEY'RE ALL I HAVE LEFT AND I REFUSE TO FORGET THEM.

I'M UP LATE HATING MYSELF AGAIN

I woke up looking for you.
My hand wandering through the space on
my bed
Desperate to run my hand through your
hair
When I found nothing but cold sheets my
heart panicked
Where did you go?
I sat up looking to the other side of the
bed in hopes you found your way there
But it was just me
Eventually my mind caught up with me
and I realized
You weren't there
And you never were.

My favorite
Is the pictures that hold a better time

I'm done performing.
I took my bow.
The curtains closed.
The applause has faded to nothing.
Everyone has left.
It's just me in the dark.
So why can't I stop pretending to be
someone I'm not.

Is this the Encore?

I THINK WE SHOULD NORMALIZE SOME BROKEN
THINGS STAYING BROKEN.

MUSIC MAY PASS THE TIME BUT IT GIVES THE SOUL A FEW MORE YEARS AND OPPORTUNITIES TO LICK LIFE.

I HOPE THE MUSIC GIVES THE CHILDREN MORE TIME.

When did eating become such a chore?
When did I become a risk?
It's not my fault.
I tried really hard
But in the end I told myself tomorrow
Despite my body screaming today
And I layed in bed
And hid the pain in hours of sleep

Why am I incapable of this?

My only motive for leaving my room is in hopes someone notices I need help.

PLEASE JUST LET ME GO
I CAN'T LIVE PINNED TO THE GROUND
I'M MEANT FOR THE SKY

I'm in the car on my way home
Everyone has gone their own way
The lights have been turned off
And somehow my brain knows what
nightmare is waiting to devour me at
home
That life I carried gets sucked out the
window
Blown away by the wind
I rummage my mind for something waiting
for me once I arrive
But I pull into the driveway and the lights
in my house are off as well
The door is even locked
I enter into the still, dark home
Some people go home drained
I go home desperate for more
Because without distractions
There's a monster waiting to worm its way
into my head
Fill the empty space left by no one
I wander
Trying to ignore the pain in my stomach
and the cries it makes
I lay in my bed
Even in June its cold
And I lay on my side

AND SCROLL THE INTERNET
LETTING MY BRAIN ROT AND FILL ITSELF WITH
ANYTHING THAT WILL SAVE ME
THE IDEA OF GOING TO BED FEELING THIS SAD
AND EMPTY MAKES IT ALL WORSE
BUT GOING TO BED WILL PUT ME OUT OF MISERY
I SPEND THE NEXT FEW HOURS ARGUING WITH
MYSELF OVER IT
EVENTUALLY I REACH SELF DESTRUCTION
AND CONSIDER CRYING
BUT I DON'T WANT MY HEAD TO HURT
ITS THE LEAST I CAN DO FOR MY BODY
I RUN IDEAS OF WHATS WRONG WITH ME
THROUGH MY HEAD
AND EVENTUALLY
MY SAVING GRACE
I DECIDE IT'S TIME TO PUT THE NIGHT AWAY AND
REST
MY HEAD IS FULL AND MY STOMACH IS EMPTY
AND I PRAY TOMORROW NIGHT WILL BE KINDER
TO ME

TUESDAY NIGHT

IT'S NOT THE EUTHANASIA THAT'S SAD
IT'S THE FACT THAT THEY'RE BEING
EUTHANASIAED FOR NOT BEING LOVED, TOO
LONG.

I LIKE TO THINK THAT OUT THERE
SOMEWHERE, SOMEHOW
YOU'RE STILL THERE
YELLING FOR ME DOWNSTAIRS
CALLING MY NAME THROUGH THE CROWDS
TELLING ME YOUR STORIES
AND EVEN SINGING YOUR FAVORITE SONGS
BUT I COULD BE WRONG
IT COULD JUST BE SOMETHING IN THE WIND
THAT PUTS THOSE IDEAS IN MY HEAD

I SEND THOSE LONG PARAGRAPHS AT 3AM
AS IF THE NIGHT WILL KEEP THEM QUIET
AS IF THE DARKNESS WILL HIDE MY SHAME
AND MAYBE I'LL FORGET ABOUT IT JUST FOR A
LITTLE WHILE
JUST UNTIL THE SUN RISES

People ask me why I believe in God
Why I believe in something you can't see
And I understand the confusion in their
heads
Sometimes I feel it too
But to be honest
Why not
It doesn't hurt
It feels good to believe in some higher
power loving me unconditionally
Saving me a seat in the after life
Preserving my loved ones
Always forgiving my wrongs
Guiding me through this world
And not just me
But everyone else
It's like a kid believing in magic
It gives them hope in a dark world
And it hurts no one
So why not believe in God

It's such a dark world

I just need some hope
And it feels so good

I FULLY BELIEVE IN BEING YOURSELF
BECAUSE IT'S THE ONLY WAY YOU COULD TRULY
BE HAPPY

I DISLIKED WHEN MY BEST FRIEND TALKED TO
HIGHLY OF SOMEWHERE ELSE
AND IT WASN'T BECAUSE I THOUGHT WHERE WE
WERE WAS BETTER
OR THAT SHE SHOULD APPRECIATE WHERE SHE
WAS WITH WHAT SHE HAD
I JUST DIDN'T WANT HER TO LEAVE
I DIDN'T WANT TO LOSE SOMEONE TO GREENER
HILLS AGAIN
AND MAYBE THAT MAKES ME SELFISH

THEY WERE MORE OF AN ADULT THAN THEY
SHOULD HAVE BEEN.

They say sisters are tied souls
Forever together through this life
Always finding a way through hard times
Hand in hand
They say if you were going to have anyone
it would be her
They were the friends that would last a
lifetime
I suppose our lifetime was cut short
Cause you're not here
Like two souls cut in half
But I think you took a piece of mine with
you
Because you made it so anyone was capable
of walking away.
And any ounce of faith or security I had
in anyone was gone too.

Her middle name was Grace

Isn't it sad that in order for us to
convince people to be kind
We must promise kindness in return

Comfort without sacrifice

WHERE DID I GO?
HOW DID I GET HERE WITHOUT HER?

I ALWAYS CONNECTED WITH YOU THROUGH
HEARTBREAK
AND DISASTERS
NOW YOU SING OF LOVE
YOU'VE GROWN AND CHANGED
AND EVEN THOUGH I LOVE TOO
I STILL YEARN FOR THE MISERY WE BOTH FELT

THERE IS SOMETHING GLORIOUS ABOUT THE WAY
YOU BREAK

I'M NOT A POET
I THINK THERE'S JUST SOMEONE LIVING IN MY
HEAD
BUT MAYBE THAT IS WHAT MAKES A POET?

I SHOULD BE GRATEFUL I DIDN'T BECOME A
MONSTER?

I CAN'T FIND A WAY TO EXPLAIN TO PEOPLE THAT
I JUST WANT TO LEAVE.
I WANT TO FIND OTHER WORLDS
AND ONLY CONSIDER COMING HOME.

TRAVELER

I STOPPED SEEING YOU
I STOPPED TEXTING YOU
I STOPPED LOOKING AT THE PHOTOS OF YOU
I STOPPED TALKING ABOUT YOU
I STOPPED DOING THE THINGS WE DID
TOGETHER
I EVEN STOPPED WRITING ABOUT YOU
I DID EVERYTHING TO GET RID OF YOU

HOW ARE YOU STILL BREAKING MY HEART?
HOW ARE YOU GETTING IN?
HOW DO I GET YOU OUT?

I OFTEN WAKE UP WITH HEADACHES.
WHAT WAS HAUNTING ME IN MY SLEEP?

I'M AFRAID TO LET YOU INTO MY MIND
I DON'T WANT TO LOSE THE CONTROL I HAVE
OVER HOW YOU SEE ME.

I'll always be there to help you
And maybe
I'll either learn to help myself
Or find someone willing to return the
favor

ICARUS WAS MADE OUT TO BE A FOOL
BUT HE WAS JUST A BOY PAYING FOR HIS FATHERS
CRIMES
DESPERATE TO BE WITH WHO HE LOVED
BEGGING FOR MERCY
HE WASN'T BOASTING
HE WASN'T IGNORANT
THIS ISN'T A METAPHOR THAT SAYS TO NOT GO
TOO FAR OR YOU'LL BURN
ICARUS KNEW WHAT WOULD HAPPEN
BUT HE WAS STILL BRAVE ENOUGH TO DO IT
ANYWAY
DESPITE THE RISK OF DYING
HE WASN'T A FOOL
HE JUST WANTED TO LIVE

I looks at the words I fell in love with
years ago
I was desperate to know how to say
goodbye
And I suppose I learned
Because I'm not her anymore
And I no longer love the words I was
devoted to

THE SKY IS MISSING AND THE STARS HAVE FALLEN
INTO OUR EYES.

She's so full of lies
She's ignorant and she's hard to handle
She doesn't know when to quit
She just keeps going and going
Always in places she shouldn't be
She's reckless not just with herself but
with the people around her.
And I wish I could dig her out
Remove her from myself
Because she hurts me so fucking bad
And I'm tired of wasting tears on her
I'm sick of her ruining my life
I fear it will get so bad
I will crack open my ribs
And tear her from the center of myself
Even if it means
I go down with her

I'VE NEVER BEEN GOOD AT LETTING THINGS GO. THIS IS PROBABLY BECAUSE WHENEVER I REACHED WITH MY HAND, I WAS NEVER UNDER THE IMPRESSION THAT I'D EVER HAVE TO RELEASE MY GRASP.

IS IT REAL?
OR AM I TRYING TO KILL MYSELF AGAIN?

THERE IS THIS PAIN WITHIN MYSELF
AND I DON'T SEEM TO HAVE ENOUGH APOLOGIES
TO MAKE IT GO AWAY.
YOUR EYES BREAK ME
LEAVE ME BURNING FROM THE INSIDE OUT
A PIT FORMING DEEP
SO DEEP I CAN'T REACH
NOT EVEN WITH THE FANCIEST WORDS.
I'M SORRY. (IT'S NOT ENOUGH).
STILL...I AM
I'M TRYING TO REACH FOR YOU
IN HOPES TO END THE PAIN
AND I DON'T JUST MEAN MINE.
THE SOURCE OF MY PAIN IS A FRACTION OF
YOUR HEARTBREAK.

I DIDN'T HIDE.
I WANTED TO
REALLY BADLY
I WAS CLOSE TO SHUTTING EVERYONE OUT
AND I WOULD HAVE BEEN OKAY WITH THAT
EXCEPT THERE'S YOU
I PICTURE YOUR FACE
AND THAT OVERTHINKING MIND OF YOURS
AND I CAN'T BRING MYSELF TO DO IT.
IT BREAKS MY HEART MORE THAN WHAT'S
MAKING ME WANT TO HIDE.
AND SO I STAY.

I WISH YOU HAD THE SAME THOUGHT PROCESS
BEFORE YOU DECIDED TO DISAPPEAR.

I NOTICED THAT PEOPLE CARRY AROUND THESE
BURNT OUT STARS
SOME HAVE A FEW
SOME HAVE MANY
SOME HAVE MORE THAN I CAN IMAGINE
BUT SOMETHING THEY SHARE IS THEY'RE ALWAYS
CHASING A STAR THAT STILL SHINES
I LOOK AT THESE PEOPLE
AND THEN I LOOK AT MYSELF....
I DON'T HAVE A BURNT OUT STAR
I FEAR I'M FALLING BEHIND
BECAUSE MY ONE SHINING STAR SEEMS TOO
GOOD TO BE TRUE.

Do the things I say belong in the ears of others?
Are these words meant to be more than mine?
If I let them out...
How bad will it hurt when they never return to me.

I'VE ALWAYS TREASURED MY ABILITY TO NEVER GET TIRED OF THOSE WHO CANNOT STOP RUNNING.

MAYBE THE WORLD DIDN'T KNOW YOU WERE
JUST A MAN.

PRETTY LIKE GOLDEN NATURE.

SOMETIMES YOU CAN'T HELP WHAT THE WORLD
MADE YOU.

PASSION IS SOMETHING THAT REFLECTS A
FRAGMENT OF YOURSELF
AND LETTING OTHER PEOPLE SEE IT.

I was always told grief had stages
And they made it seem like you passed
through the stages
Sometimes going back to revisit stages
And eventually you leave them and Heal
But I learned.
It's not like moving from room to room
It's one long staircase going up
Collecting each stage
Each feeling
And keeping them all inside you
You don't move on from them
You learn to survive with them

Surviving is not Healing

I BELIEVE GOD STILL WEEPS FOR LUCIFER
I BELIEVE HE BEGGED FOR A WAY TO KEEP HIM
BEGGED FOR FATE TO CHANGE

One thing I hate most
Is money
It fills our heads
And empties our hands
It strips our dreams
And bends our character
This world is tainted with greed
Minds are being poisoned
People will kill for money
Because they believe it will save them
But it will only crush your soul
Money has corrupt us
It has left a stain,
Even money can't get out

I SPENT HOURS SCROLLING THROUGH
COMMENTS
PEOPLE SHARING WHAT THEY DID THAT DAY
SO MANY BEAUTIFUL RESPONSES
SOME HAPPY
SOME SIMPLE
SOME VERY SAD
BUT IT WAS STILL BEAUTIFUL
JUST TO SEE WHAT EVERYONE SPENT THEIR TIME
ON
THE SAME TIME I SPENT THAT SAME DAY
PEOPLE I DON'T KNOW
PROOF THAT THEY LIVED TODAY

You can't promise anything
Life shifts too quickly
Things break
Time moves
People are flawed
Nothing can be guaranteed
You can't promise anything
You can only promise to consider trying

I DROP TO MY KNEES
MY ARMS GO NUMB
AND I FALL INTO YOUR EMBRACE
I'VE BEEN AWAY FOR FAR TOO LONG
AND I'VE GROWN TIRED
I'VE BEEN NEEDING YOU WITHOUT KNOWING IT
THIS DESIRE TO GO HOME
HAS BEEN A DESIRE FOR MY FATHER

Much like any feeling, Love has a spectrum and fluctuates. It's gained and it is lost.

I feel like we forget that

I ALWAYS HOPE FOR SOMEONE TO LOVE THE
VILLAIN
TO CHOOSE THEM
TO HAVE FAITH IN THEM
BECAUSE I CAN'T IMAGINE THE AMOUNT OF PAIN
AND REJECTION THEY RECEIVED TO GET TO
THAT PLACE
THE LACK OF LOVE THAT FORMED THEM
AND MAYBE IF SOMEONE SEES THEM
TRULY SEES THEM
AND PICKS THEM FOR ONCE
MAYBE THEN THEY WILL LET THE LOVE IN AND
SAVE THEIR SOUL AND HEAL THOSE SHATTERED
PIECES
AND CHASE AWAY THE EVIL THAT'S BEEN STUCK
IN THEIR MINDS TO RELEASE THEIR HEARTS THAT
HAVE BEEN HELD CAPTIVE FOR SO LONG

THEY DON'T DESERVE A BEATING
THEY DESERVE TO BE LOVED

My eyes still cry and my heart still aches
I spend nights awake calling out your
name with my face pressed into the pillow.
I remember how you were here and it's still
a shock to think any differently.
Your life is gone and in a way
So is mine.

I FIND MYSELF FACE TO FACE WITH A DIMMER
SUN.

You've slipped away
And just like that
A whole world is gone

Everything

I HATE THE POWER YOU HAVE OVER ME.
THE TWIST IN MY GUT WHEN I RUN INTO YOU IN
THE STORE.
THE TWINGE IN MY BONES WHEN I HEAR YOUR
NAME
AND THAT HEART BREAK WHEN I SEE THE
PICTURES
THAT HOLD THE LIFE WE USED TO HAVE,
TOGETHER.
AND THE JOY YOU TOOK FROM ME.

NOTHING WILL TEAR YOU INTO A GREAT TWO
THAN BEING AFRAID OF WHAT YOU NEED

It feels like a one way staircase only going
down
Never finding the bottom
Spiraling around and around
Looking up to your past self
And down to only more stairs

I'm still whole without you
I didn't need you to complete me
But that doesn't mean I didn't need you
When you're whole, you feel like you're on
top of the world
But when you have someone like I did
You are so far beyond you forget what
the ground even feels like.
This never ending high and joy when
they're there.
But when they're gone
You're left on the ground with a
headache, staring up to where you used to
be
Desperately trying to figure out how to
get back up.

MY HEART REALLY HURTS
I'M THINKING OF CUTTING IT OUT

You can fall in love with a person
But you can also just fall in love with the
art and passion within them
Similar but separate loves

Inspiration vs. Infatuation

I ALWAYS DREAMT OF BECOMING A STAR
TUCKED PERFECTLY INTO THE SEA OF SKY AND
SPACE
BORN TO RADIATE PASSION AND LOVE,
WITH A GOLDEN GLOW
BURNED INTO EXISTENCE FOR GENERATIONS
BUT A PART OF ME LOOKS AT MY LIFE AND
WONDERS
PERHAPS THAT WAS A FORMER LIFE
MAYBE I WAS IN THE SKY
BUT THE LIGHT DIED OUT
AND I FELL
TRADGECIALLY
BUT NOT ENOUGH FOR ANYONE TO NOTICE
AND NOW I'M DESTINED TO WALK THE EARTH,
AND BE REMINDED EVERY NIGHT OF THE HOME I
LOST.

I WANT TO GO HOME

I don't think I'm meant for anyone
Like a martyr
I run with the torch alone
Free to set the flames without fear
Leaving only me to burn
And I think that's okay

Whenever I see your sad eyes
Caused by the homes we were raised in
I want to grab your hands
Make promises just out of a glance
and run far
Maybe Sweden....or Spain

Somewhere the sun shines brighter

LITERALLY JUST STEP ON ME AT THIS POINT

If I am to be casted out into the fields all
alone
Let me be David
If I am to be executed
Let me be Charlotte Corday
If I am to fall from the sky
Let me be icarus
If I am to lose my love
Let me be Achillis
And if I'm made for anything
Let this life be it.

Sometimes you have to lose pieces of what you should be
To become what you want to be

I PRAY FOR PEACE TO FIND YOU
I'LL PRAY TO ANY GOD THAT WILL LISTEN FOR THE PAIN TO
CONCLUDE
DESPITE BEING FLAWED AND HUMAN
YOU DON'T DESERVE TO FALL APART UNDER THE STARS
IF I COULD I'D HOLD YOU TOGETHER UNTIL THE SUN DRIED YOUR
TEARS I WOULD EVERY NIGHT
I'M SORRY THEY SAID THOSE THINGS
I'M SORRY THAT THEY FAILED YOU
AND I'M SORRY IF I DID TOO.
I AM SORRY FOR THE PAIN THAT LEAKS FROM YOUR HEAD AND
INTO YOUR HEART, BURNING YOUR LUNGS, STEALING THE BREATH
THAT THEY HOLD AND WEAKENING EVERY MUSCLE THAT HELD YOU
THROUGH THE DAY.
YOU ARE NOT WHAT YOU MIGHT THINK
YOU ARE NOT DISGUSTING
YOU ARE NO BURDEN
YOU ARE NOT STRANDED OR DESERTED
YOU ARE NOT DESERVING OF THE SUFFERING YOU FACE
YOU ARE CAPABLE
YOU ARE LOVED
YOU ARE MEANT TO BE HERE
YOU ARE SO VERY BEAUTIFUL
AND IF YOU DON'T THINK THAT IS TRUE
ALWAYS KNOW I BELIEVE IT MORE THAN I BELIEVE THE SUN IN THE
SKY
MORE THAN I BELIEVE IN THE STARS
MORE THAN THE GRASS ON THE GROUND
MORE THAN THE DARK NIGHT
AND THE BRIGHT SKIES
AND MORE THAN I BELIEVE IN ANYTHING YOU COULD FATHOM

THIS IS FOR YOU

Are you slipping my words into your lyrics again?

I'VE BEEN PRAISED FOR BEING VERY
THOUGHTFUL
SPENDING MUCH OF MY TIME THINKING OF
HOW I COULD BENEFIT OTHERS
PUTTING IMMENSE DETAIL INTO MY LOVE FOR
THEM
LEAVING NO ROOM FOR DOUBT
BUT THIS CAN BE DAMAGING
SPENDING SO MUCH TIME, ENERGY, LOVE, AND
THOUGHT ON SOMEONE ONLY TO RECEIVE SUCH
LITTLE IN RETURN
I SHOWED YOU ALL THE LOVE I HAD TO GIVE
AND I GOT A GLIMPSE IN RETURN
I UNDERSTAND ITS NOT SOMETHING EVERYONE
CAN GIVE SO FREELY
I JUST WISH I COULD HOLD ONTO MY LOVE IN
THE MEANTIME
TO NOT FEEL SO OFF BALANCED
AND UNLOVED.

I NEVER WANT ANYONE TO DOUBT MY LOVE FOR
THEM
BECAUSE I KNOW HOW DAMAGING THAT CAN
FEEL

I LOVE YOU TOO

My heart fears the day it does not have
you
Where will it go?
It will be left to wonder lost
Or be locked inside my chest

That is no life for a heart like mine

I was laying in the snow
Except the snow started to melt beneath me
Revealing the hard cement
It was dark out
There was a silence only the snow banks could give you
The glow of the orange streetlight shined over me
Big fluffy flakes showered down almost in slow motion
Dropping onto my face sending a kiss of cold into my skin.
There was peace despite bleeding out
It's really beautiful
It was pouring out at a rate that left me to savor the
moment.
I could feel the warmth filling the back of my throat
Coming up and out through my cough
I could have yelled for help but I didn't want to disrupt
the silent air
I thought about what was going to happen to me
I didn't want this but I think I've still accepted it
Tears started to form in the corners of my eyes, quickly
falling down the side of my face and into my ear
I thought about my father, his twisted face when he sees
me again
I think he might cry
He might even pray
I can feel by clothes begin to soak in the crimson red
I think about my time
How much I have left
How much I had
And what I did with it
My lungs feel heavy and it burns
This cold air still finds it way to them
The tears have formed a constant stream
I think about who I should have hugged harder
But it doesn't really mean anything, does it?
I think the ground will hold me the tightest
My body starts to shake from the dense air grasping to my
limbs

MY MOTHER WOULD HAVE GOTTEN ME A BLANKET
SHE STILL COULD, MAYBE NOT OF COTTON, BUT PETALS
MY BREATH IS LOUDER, STAGGERING, IT'S GETTING HARDER
MY LUNGS ARE FIGHTING FOR A BREATH BUT MY LIMBS ARE STILL
AND RELAXED, LIKE THEY ARE ALREADY GONE.
I TWITCH MY FINGER TO ENSURE THEY'RE STILL THERE, OR MAYBE
TO FEEL SOMETHING AND HOLD ONTO WHAT IT FEELS LIKE. IT
FINDS MY BLOOD.
NEARLY NUMB I STILL FIND THE WARMTH AND SILK TOUCH
THE STREET LIGHT AND COLD WIND BEGINS TO TIRE MY EYES,
CREATING A PAIN LIKE SMALL SCRAPES AGAINST THE SURFACE.
I SQUEEZE THEM TIGHT, CREATING TENSION WITHIN MY SKIN,
CAUSING A WAVE OF TEARS TO EXIT THE HALLOWS OF MY EYE.
QUICKLY I OPEN THEM TO FACE THE SKY JUST A LITTLE MORE
YOU CANT SEE THE SKY IF YOU'RE IN IT
IT'S REALLY PRETTY....ITS SO PRETTY
IT'S GETTING DARKER
THE COLD HAS NUMBED THE EXTERIOR PAIN
WHAT SHOULD MY LAST THOUGHT BE?
WHAT IS DESERVING OF MY FINAL MINUTES?
I RUN MY MIND THROUGH MOMENTS AND PEOPLE
WHERE DID I GO WHEN I WAS ALIVE?
I'VE SUDDENLY FORGOTTEN
I DON'T MIND
I'LL SETTLE FOR NOW.
IT'S REALLY BEAUTIFUL.

My Dear Silvia
You are by far the loveliest
Even your name on my tongue
The dark auburn that coats your skin
shines like the sun was made for it
And when I think you reached all beauty
You sing with such vibrancy
A deep tone that shakes my bones and
resonates with my heart.

ADDICTION ISN'T ALWAYS A CHOICE
LOSING THE TRUST OF THE PEOPLE YOU LOVE
AND LOSING YOURSELF ISN'T SOMETHING A
PERSON CHOOSES
SOMETIMES IT'S THE AFTERMATH OF SOMETHING
SO EXCRUCIATING AND UNBEARABLE
AND IT LEAVES YOU WITH NOTHING EXCEPT A
SUBSTANCE THAT WILL EASE THE PAIN FOR EVEN
JUST A MOMENT

SOME RELIEF IS WORTH THE WHOLE WORLD

WE CAN'T ALWAYS STAY STRONG

THE DREAMS TOOK MY HEAD AGAIN
IT WON'T BE SOON BUT THEY WILL RETURN WITH
IT
SOME DAYS I WISH THEY'D NEVER COME HOME
WITH IT
MY HEAD IS LIGHTER WITHOUT IT.

That sad feeling held me the tightest
growing up
Maybe that's why I give in so easily to the
emotion
Let it consume me
I search for it in the night
I pull it from its hiding place and bury it
into my chest
It gives me this nostalgic feeling
Something like home
It makes me feel something
Strong and familiar
There is no surprise when it comes to
sorrow
Comfort in the stillness
A hug from a childhood friend I spent
many nights with
When I had nothing else

SOMETIMES I NEED LOVE FROM SOMEONE WHO
ISN'T OBLIGATED TO GIVE IT TO ME

I'M NOT SURE WHAT LEVEL OF GIVING UP I'M
WILLING TO DO

HE WAS SLOWLY STRIPPED OF EVERYTHING HE
HAD
I TOOK ADVANTAGE OF THE PEOPLE AROUND
HIM
HE HURT THEM BECAUSE HE DIDN'T THINK HE
NEEDED THEM.
HE ASSUMED THEY WOULD ALWAYS NEED HIM.
AND NOW THAT HE HAS NOTHING AND THEY
HAVE EVERYTHING.
HE HAS TO ADMIT HE WAS WRONG.
HE HAS TO ADMIT HE NEEDS HELP
OR HE WILL SUFFER ALONE FOREVER.

CHIEF WITHOUT A TRIBE

THE SUN PROMISED ME PARADISE
BUT HAS ONLY DELIVERED BURNS
IT HAS CASTED ME OUT OF THE SKY
TO BECOME A SLAVE IN THE GROUND
I JUST WANTED TO FEEL THE HEAVENS

I THOUGHT YOU COULD NEVER LEAVE THIS
WORLD WITHOUT ME IF I HELD YOU TIGHT
ENOUGH
AND IT WASN'T MY GRIP THAT FAILED ME
IT WAS THE LOOK IN YOUR EYES THAT SAID "LET
GO."
YOU SQUEEZED MY HAND AND LOOSENED YOUR
GRIP
AND A NEW GRIP GRABBED A HOLD OF ME
PEOPLE BEGGING ME TO STAY
BECAUSE THEY DIDN'T WANT ME TO LEAVE THIS
WORLD WITHOUT THEM.

CIRCLE OF LOSS

SOMETIMES I'M LOST
OTHER TIMES I'M PERFECTLY FOUND

I WANT TO SURROUND MYSELF WITH BEAUTY
AND ART
I WANT IT TO BURN INTO MY HEART
AND STAIN MY BONES
I WANT TO DROWN IN IT EVERY NIGHT
I WANT IT TO LIVE IN MY MIND LIKE LUCID
DREAMS
TO LIVE BOLDLY DRENCHED IN DELUSION
I WANT THE AIR TO BE EUPHORIC AND MIND
ALTERING
TO TWIST MY SENSE AND TEAR AT MY SKIN
I WANT TO DANCE IN THE RAIN
DROPS FULL OF SORROW AND SKY
I WANT TO BE WRAPPED IN RIBBONS AND
FABRICS
TWISTED IN COLOR
FREE AT LAST

I WORKED HARD TO LOVE AND BE PROUD OF MY
LIFE
YOU DON'T GET TO HAVE IT BECAUSE YOU
NEGLECT YOURS
THIS IS MY LIFE
NOT SOMETHING YOU CAN TAKE

She wanted to save her people from bloodshed
Avenge those who fell victim in September
She knew she would die for what she did
But it was worth more than her life
She was scared but she still held her head high as she walked up the screaming wooden steps
She thought of her father
She saved 100,000 people for the cost of one
She was pretty and young
Full of anger and passion
She regretted nothing when she faced the crowd
She was proud of every moment
She even loved the sight of the bloody water
Like it was a piece of art she crafted
She was a hero
She begged for her story to be remembered just right
But they twisted her words
Tore down her humanity
And created a monster who slayed a man

Charlotte

DON'T SHOVE YOUR LIFE DOWN MY THROAT
I LEFT FOR A REASON
AND IT WASN'T TO SUFFOCATE AGAIN

Maybe the reason you run so much
Is because you're lost
Or you think you're behind
You don't deserve that
You deserve to run because you're free
Because you like the wind in your hair
And that burn in your chest
Because it makes you feel alive
You don't deserve to be trapped in fear

They took his mind
Like it wasn't his to have
They turned him into a man
He wasn't made to be
They wiped away the people who brought
him home
They made him do things that would kill
what he truly deserved.
They made a man into a monster

I PULL THE KNIVES OUT OF MY BACK
NOT TO HURT YOU WITH
BUT TO KEEP
JUST IN CASE, ONE DAY
I ACTUALLY DESERVE THEM

They were right when they said I would
feel better
Not because the weight of what you did
hurts any less
But because my head has made room for
new things
Things that don't hurt so much
Leaving less room for what you did.
So it didn't get better, what you did didn't
lessen
It's just being buried in the new life I found
without you.

YOUR HEART HURTS AND SO DOES MINE
I'LL HOLD YOU IF YOU HOLD ME
WE DON'T HAVE TO BE IN LOVE TO SHOW EACH
OTHER THE LOVE WE DESERVE

Drown me and watch me breathe
Toss me over a ledge and watch me soar
Do your best and I will still find my way
Because death is not my end
I will live on even with my name on a
stone

My head is slipping away again.
I hope to a better place.

CHANGE IS DIFFICULT BUT SOMETIMES IT IS A
SIGN THE WORLD IS STILL SPINNING

I LIKE LOOKING AT RENAISSANCE ART TO KNOW
THAT EVEN CENTURIES BEFORE ME
SOMEONE FELT THE PAIN TOO

I CAN'T BE AFRAID TO SHARE MY WORDS
JUST BECAUSE THEY FOUND PAPER DOESN'T
MEAN THE WEIGHT IS LIFTED
EXPRESSION FREES YOU FROM SELF OPPRESSION

I HAVE TO TRUST THAT I'M RIGHT WHERE I'M
SUPPOSED TO BE.

I CALLED YOU MINE TODAY
WHO WOULD'VE THOUGHT THAT WOULD BE
SUCH A SILLY MISTAKE.

MAYBE WE WERE MADE TO BREAK
BUT DESTINED TO HEAL.

HONEY, HEAVEN CAN WAIT FOR US.

FOREVER YOUNG

I'VE SEEM TO HAVE FORGOTTEN THE PASSION I
HAD.
WAS IT TRULY PASSION IF I FORGOT IT SO EASILY?
OR IS PASSION NOT AS POWERFUL AS I THOUGHT?

MAYBE I WAS LACED WITH DELUSION.

MAYBE PASSION WAS A LIE TO CONVINCE US WE
WERE GIFTED.

I CAN'T KEEP LIVING THE WAY I HAVE BEEN.
NOT FOREVER

In the beginning I wasn't sure if I was allowed to love you.
Now I'm not sure if I'm allowed to not love you.

It's like holding onto a shard of glass
It digs into your flesh
And the soul and love I have pours out of
me
The blood stains the floor
And the pain carries on
Grasping tightly as to not let the shard
fall
And break more than it already is

"ACCEPT YOUR LIFE THE WAY IT IS"
BULLSHIT
IF YOU DON'T LOVE YOUR LIFE
CHANGE IT
AND DON'T STOP TRYING UNTIL IT'S JUST RIGHT
YOU ONLY LIVE ONCE
DON'T SETTLE FOR LIVING AN UNSATISFYING
LIFE
IT'S NOT RIGHT
IT'S NOT HUMANE TO SUFFER WITH EVERY
BREATH

I FEEL LIKE OUT OF ALL THE THINGS WE
UNDERSTAND
OURSELVES SHOULD AT LEAST BE ONE OF THEM.

WHEN WILL I STOP BEING PUNISHED FOR
FEELINGS I COULD NOT FEEL?
WHEN WILL I STOP BEING THE FACE OF THE
MONSTER THAT KEPT YOU UP AT NIGHT?
WHEN WILL PEOPLE STOP DROWNING ME IN THE
WORDS THAT BROKE ME EVERY NIGHT?
I WANTED THE PAIN TO END JUST AS MUCH AS
YOU.
I SHOULD NOT HAVE TO SUFFER FOR THE
NIGHTMARES I DID NOT FUEL.
I WANT IT TO END
BECAUSE I'M GETTING CLOSER TO RECOGNIZING
THE HORRIBLE PERSON IN THE MIRROR.

I MIGHT BE TOO BLINDED BY SELFISH DESIRES TO
DESERVE LOVE

I DON'T EVEN TRUST MYSELF.

DO I REALLY BELIEVE STARVING WILL SAVE ME?

My sadness sickens me

THERE ARE A LOT OF WORDS IN MY HEAD
THEY'RE MOVING AND TWISTING TOGETHER
AND STARTING TO NOT MAKE MUCH SENSE

You can't hold onto me for too long
I belong to the sky

I BELIEVE THAT WE WERE MADE FOR EACH OTHER
LIKE A CAGE FOR A BIRD

I WANTED TO BE FREE

THESE AREN'T JUST WORDS
THEY'VE NEVER BEEN JUST WORDS

DOES THERE COME A POINT WHERE WANTING TO
AVOID SUFFERING ISN'T SELFISH?
IS IT SELFISH IF I JUST WANT TO SAVE MYSELF
JUST ONCE
JUST THIS ONE TIME

WHEN DOES SELFISH BECOME SELF CARE

I JUST WANTED TO MAKE IT HOME ONE LAST TIME.

I'M ASHAMED OF MYSELF
EVERYTHING SHORT OF PERFECT

I'M NOT ENTIRELY SURE WHAT IT COSTS TO LIVE
IN THIS WORLD.
TO BE A PERSON.
BUT WHAT I CAN TELL YOU
IS THAT IT'S NOT WORTH A FRACTION OF WHAT
I'VE PAID.

WHAT IT TAKES TO BE HUMAN

I KNOW IT SEEMS HOPELESS
AND YOU WANT TO BE QUICK TO END IT
BUT HOLD ONTO ME FOR JUST THE NIGHT
AND WE'LL LET TIME GO ON WITHOUT US
AND WE'LL SIT UNTIL THE SUN COMES UP AND
WE'LL FIND HOPE IN IT
I PROMISE
AND IF I HAVE TO HOLD YOU TOMORROW NIGHT
AND EVEN FOREVER
I WILL
JUST STAY WITH ME AND WATCH THE SUN COME
UP
I'LL HOLD YOU UNTIL THE SUN SHINES ON US

I PROMISE, I PROMISE, I PROMISE, I PROMISE

I DON'T THINK WE APPRECIATE THOSE PEOPLE
WHO NEVER GIVE UP ON US, AS MUCH AS WE
SHOULD

THANK YOU FOR NOT GIVING UP ON ME

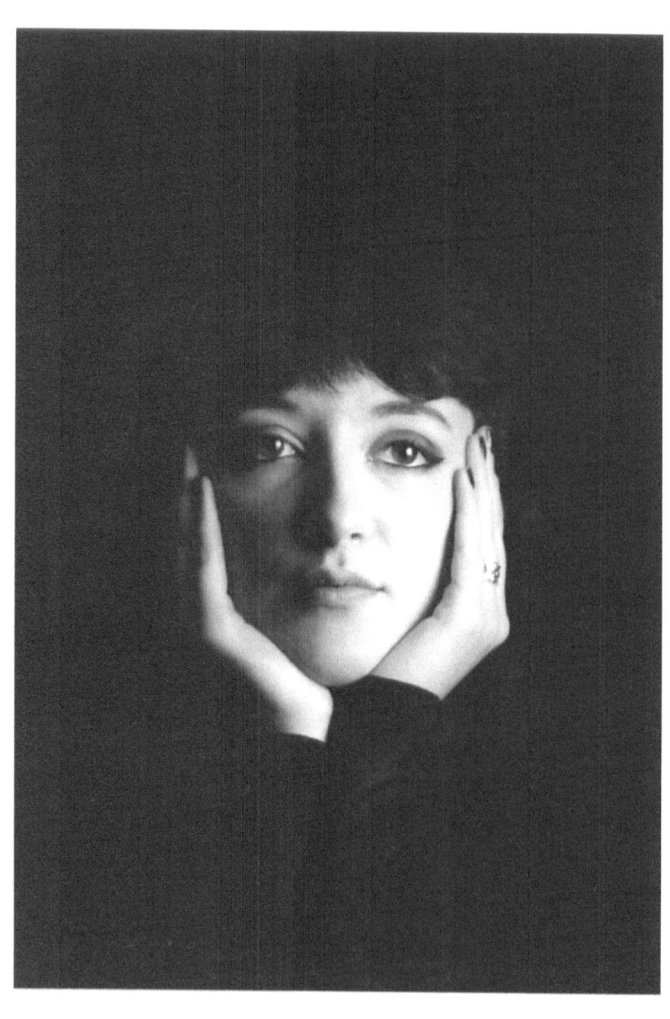

I AM STILL DEAD, I PROMISE.

978-1-300-91715-1
Imprint: Lulu.com